A. F. MORITZ

Mahoning

Brick Books

CANADIAN CATALOGUING IN PUBLICATION DATA

Moritz, A.F.
　Mahoning

Poems.
ISBN 0-919626-73-4

1. Title.

PS8576.O724M3 1994　　C811'.54　　C94-931965-1
PR9199.3.M67M3 1994

Copyright © A.F. Moritz, 1994.

The support of the Canada Council and the Ontario Arts Council is gratefully acknowledged. The support of the Government of Ontario through the Ministry of Culture, Tourism and Recreation is also gratefully acknowledged.

Cover and author photos by Theresa Moritz.
Interior photos by Albert F. Moritz.

Typeset in Trump Mediaeval. Printed and bound by The Porcupine's Quill. The stock is acid-free Zephyr Antique laid.

Brick Books
Box 20081, 431 Boler Road
London, Ontario
N6K 4G6

... dona laboratae Cereris ...
    – Vergil, *Aeneid* VIII

(... which earth has given and human hands have made ...)

... verde sueño
del suelo gris y de la parda tierra,
agria melancolía
de la ciudad decrépita,
me habéis llegado al alma,
¿o acaso estabais en el fondo de ella?
    – Antonio Machado, 'Campos de Soria'

(... green dream of the gray soil and parched earth, bitter sadness of the decrepit city, have you newly come into my soul, or have you always been there in the depths of it?)

Why should I move from this place
where I was born? knowing
how futile would be the search
for you in the multiplicity
of your debacle. The world spreads
for me like a flower opening ...
    – W.C. Williams, *Paterson*

TABLE OF CONTENTS

Part 1: Egypt

    Egypt (sections I-XI)   11

Part 2: The Traveller

    The Two Cities   25
    I Saw You Exult   26
    Near Ravenna   27
    The Gifts   28
    Le Paresseux   30
    The Traveller   31
    Entrance to Tivoli   32

Part 3: City Plan

    Morning, Loneliness Died   35
    City Plan   36
    Along the Rails   40
    Secrecy   41
    Our Sister   42
    Stoplights   43
    Fresh Grave   44
    Omniscience   45
    On a Screen   46
    Waiting for a Parade   47

Part 4: Founders

    Visit Home   51
    First   54
    East Wall   55
    Shade   56
    One With the Sun   58
    Kingdom and Leaves   60
    Evening   61
    Centuries Ago   63
    Founders   64
    The Upper Stories   66

Part 5: The Faithful One

    The Faithful One (sections I-XV)   69

Part 6: Following the Mahoning

    Given   87
    In Niles   89
    Factory Shell   91
    A Praise   92
    Road into Warren: Shift Change   96
    The Meander   98
    Mosquito Creek   99
    Bonham Woods, Bank of the Mosquito   101
    That You Still Live   103
    Country Near Lake Milton   105
    Lost Content   107

Notes and Acknowledgements   109

I

Egypt

I

I wake up. And it seems to me I am
in childhood's place again – or still:
that the far-off Mahoning flows nearby,
while heat and floating water gather
and thicken in September's night:
summer should be over, dead,
but it rages one more time, and in the fever
that starts in summer's sleep and breaks its dream,
making it wake to this oppression,
the crickets are vibrating, their steady drills
not music but something older, cool
and clear: sweet water at its source, in the midst
of burnt water: this suffocating night like a covering
of doused ash, sodden but still fiery.

Silence or the crickets' voice contrives to sparkle
in blackness, and wind makes its fresh water sound in leaves.
Now again as at first: I am in an upstairs bedroom,
skin suffering and hearing blessed
in the humid dark, and surrounding heads of maple trees
that bring the river-like voice I seem to know
screen me away from my river. It's as if the wall
that the world is were a graceful labyrinth
of leaves and branches, inviting
endless transgression: openings, entrances
everywhere, and numberless winding ways
leading to forkings into other ways, the same.
It's as if a voice gave me the key, saying,
'Walk through the wall,' and I went,
it was permeable like mist or night,
but it goes on and on, maybe the thickness
of that intangible wall is without an end.

II

I wake up. The summer is almost dead,
but still from dead of night it's far till dawn,
when light will show whether the heat-broken dream
has taken me back and I'm by the Mahoning again.
Then I'll see its horizons: the low hills
and distant ridges violet with factory smoke
that melts into low blue clouds, and blooms of flame
from long black mills on the river flats
in the narrow valley. Closer, a railroad embankment cuts
a flowering swamp, and the rails end
in the millyard of the Republic Works: truck cartons
and boxcars wait, locked,
by the rusted sheet-metal office hut
and very near, just beyond the chain-link fence
topped with barbed wire, is the wealthy ditch:
still water, purple aster,
goldenrod, yarrow, a droning of cicadas,
dragonflies and crickets – my world between
the fence and the highway's crumbling asphalt edge.

Who are you, who are known in
mating dragonflies moored to a milkweed stalk? In the night
shifts flooding into black hangars under vapour lights.
In the archetype – a famous photograph – of a helmeted
and goggled man bent by his shovel's weight,
the two of them together forming one black silhouette,
a precise, empty shape, against the white flaring
of a molten metal stream. In the Cyclopean
corpses of dead technologies a new god
long ago murdered: blast furnace, open hearth,
the Bessemer converter that sent its orange dawn
all night for decades promising eternity
out of the Mahoning's valley at Brier Hill.
Who are you, and what was all that for,
so that you tolerated it a little while
in the vast indifference of your love?

III

The vast indifference of your love.
Yet they sank their faces between those earthen mounds,
their body in dusk grasses, in never-broken shade,
eating white dust or rot.

The storm struck – gale, downpour, flood.
A deer was swept from a ledge and you felt your heart beat.
Lightning flashed out again, again, each second
throughout the northern sky all night, lashing the swamps
and hillsides of burnt, broken trunks smoking under the rain.
Wind ruffled the fires, spread a smell of sodden ash.

You felt your heart beat: the thunder
pounded on their breasts all night, obscuring the heartbeats
of animals and men. For the fury to pass,
they stared, impassive, beaten, waiting,

dwarfed.

IV

They never spoke to you.
And out in the world, before they entered you,
they had never heard you spoken of, only named.
Then we forged into you, and the silence there –
silence not silence but the stir of leaves
to the wind, the finch, the fox, and ravelling of water
under ridges in a dark noon with the crack and clatter
of a dead branch falling through branches –
the lack of words pleased us. Deep in you,
devoid of words, we found a thing to say:

What need is there for speech except to measure
planks, heaps, furnaces? We are left alone here
as if only the stirring, in night, in death, of seeds
under rotted leaves, and never to be more.
But our life is not wood but the fire
we make starring this darkness, is this first
furnace we called Maria on the Mosquito's bank,
and the five poor tons of spongy iron it gives
each day: first of the goods that we will send
flowing away without end on sparkling rivers.

People without more ceremony than that. We forged
a bowel into you, we were the new, iron bowel
lying within the dark of your leaves and steep ridges.
Our sign: smoke. We burnt you to feed
the distant lighted skin, the head and face
that crawled with vacant pleasures – to feed
New York and Washington with iron. And we were happy,
proud to be silent, proud to be no more
than the organ New York floated upon, ashamed,
the power in Washington's false step,
a filthy ancestor in California's forgotten tree.

V

You saw nothing, built nothing, dance of leaves.
Brown bodies fallen under light
lay down in noon, a shade as deep as night,
in peace sweet-scented with their own decay.

There
and also through grasses wilting on a naked rise,
through frozen burning, the snow shroud, through a whole world,
you, transformed to mud barrens, the early spring,
went the first men and women along their endless roads
one footstep wide between thorns that trace
the million profiles of your waters.

We saw them retreating, a glance, a light
reflected from a bare shoulder, and we chased,
we followed them: the people of red clay,
of salt and the beaver. But did not catch them:
they died in flight: in you
the brown bodies fell
as into their own breast
and somewhere here lie buried.

VI

Then with our hands we scooped out fish
from the full river, Mahoning,
and heaped them: enough caught in a day
to feed the town all winter. Elm and oak,
chestnut and maple shaded a paltry naked place
razed from the forest, littered with stumps,
around the courthouse of local stone.

You were matchless in remote beauty,
in slowness of dying,
in bitter pride,
the demand to be remembered and praised above all.
Not as earth, but this earth, Mahoning's land,
matchless in beauty that freezes, cracks and burns,
unseen, unheard, scraping itself away.

Buried in you, dispersed in coal and ore
and fires not yet lit: numberless bells, unforged,
untuned, untimed, chiming for the far-off.

Your body buried in the bodies
of the people buried in you, your voice
in their stolid throats.

VII

Hold back your fury and let us be.

Your peace too is fury. Hold back
the din of locusts, the mosquito swarm,
the burning and rotting in the wood and the sun.

Temper the silence when snow of its own weight
releases a cedar branch to spring back to the sky
and falls,
startling the otters at play,
on muscular, many-knotted ice
that shows how the unhurried running of your blood
froze, stiff and white.

Unexhausted one, your blood
always running within the beautiful dead stream,
white-sheathed, or in the same stream
green and agile
being reborn.

VIII

How much pleasure is in your burning:
as much as will be in your snow.
Tulle of ice on your thighs,
veil of marsh mist across your navel.

Dying is what you are but you leapt and ran along
the sloped meadows with nothing of death in you.
You flashed on the brown ridges and creek beds,
the cities' blinding gray. You broke
in a storm's wrecking vigour. Lightning
branched out, the contradictory flow of your power, a river
that creates and fills its tributaries,
driving them through the whole sky.
Every second: a new system of streams made and destroyed
for all of a September night. Scent of ozone.
Soft, sparse rain at first that crept closer
in the huge air tearing itself apart.
Then the air, stunned. The drowning rain, muscular,
on beaten grasses, on the new-made, submissive mud.

'I will be this destruction to its end.'
Your furious voice, living steel, after the storm
all around us nevertheless was fainter.
'I, I alone, could have shown you cities
worthy to live and die in.'

IX

Glory faithfully squandered, the rain sounds, vagrant savours,
the last winds tearing apart
dead storm clouds painted with evening colours now
compared to molten metals as once to animal blood.

And memory squandered, day by day, running placid or enraged
under the lip of earth, forgotten, under maples, tar and wheat.

You laughed at the fading
of a cloud shaped like a country of wooded ridges,
river valleys, towns and mills, as it withered
and dissolved, exhausted,
to be remade into something else, drifting east.
In that cloud, a thing so small, for an afternoon
driven scourged across your sky,
you were forever unchanging.

We loved your water falling, running down.

We loved your scorn, your burnt fury.

Glory faithfully squandered. No one rested, no one ever could be satisfied
in each eternity of your corrosive days.

X

When I first saw you, you were crying,
kissing the empty sockets of coal and ore,
an abandoned factory, haunt of mourning doves,
with its wall of a thousand broken windows.
And near us was the sizzling of one last word
in an ancient neon sign, almost burnt out,
the glowing of one light through silver maple leaves
on a street of unpainted houses.
Your lips brushed the sunken drum in the marsh,
the smoke, corroded mills, glass sown in the bank.

And I thought that this was your face but you
were elsewhere: these birds, these creeks, these fields,
the same history but transformed
by a purer love, with the same beauty
but a body that does not will its own death.

XI

A child the day before, my eyes
buried contented and unknowing in the eye
of cat, snake, goldfinch, or in the pure might
of the mile-long factories, I woke up.
September dawn was burning, the colour of rust,
of drying blood, and my blood was
erect and on fire. Do what I would,
it charged and recharged its milky brilliance,
and everything fell away from me – the creek, the forest,
flower and bird, mill, metal – in restless disturbances,
my bright and dark eruptions. That day I went
and everywhere saw the rust, on rails,
fences, cars, hinges, hammers, barrels,
barges, factory walls – and knew that it was iron
escaping its alloys, returning its oxygen.
It seemed then that there must be a new purity,
a new sharpness of the air, a deeper breath
somewhere in our atmosphere. The decay
all around me: wasn't it feeding the earth?
So that beyond the depopulating smelters,
emptying stores, fraying outskirts, somewhere
there must be Egypt – another Egypt, of another river,
of a more incisive, older fear of death,
a more violent desperation, mightier tombs, and tomorrow
I would set out for new engines and fresh mills.

2

The Traveller

THE TWO CITIES

Very far now between two cities
wandering, a boy along the slate-gray
waters of the road, driftwood and crushed brown iron.
Ahead in the mirage on asphalt
his childhood tree appears once more
as on the day when it was cut,
and trembles, cries, prays
to grow tender green again and shelter.

Nothing else. In turning blackness, images not mine.
The shepherd and his flock, too real,
never seen on those ridges that melted and flowed down
to this highway, level tar.

Silver towers. Huddle of daubed huts.
If the fugitive said brick, motor, wire, rail,
were they more his, was he less a seed on pavement?
Still the mule turned in the mill, a work
flowered in the engines, in Egypt in the famished brickyard
ever farther away.

Here nothing touches or wounds. Blank, turning, alone,
in soft spaciousness, all things are infinitely far:
open hearth, stamping mill, a dead
suffering, unfelt, desiring to be
suffering again – and the holy palm,
childish willow, the spring
newly risen, blue under bright rock,
in green Egypt, her city beyond the desert tar.
When a child entered, once, its idols fell
and broke, gold pieces in a darker gold of day.
Here is the pure black road,
motionless. The step unseen.

I SAW YOU EXULT

I saw you exult as the morning grass was drying.

Then came dusty noon with its wooden poles and cables.
Cars passed down straight roads along barbed wire,
along the skeletons of rusted works,
or glinting ribs for new ones being built,
laid out in order on razed plots.

Rust stained the roots hiding in the ground,
the violet flower that ironweed
held high above the dust, even the breakers
of yarrow seething between
a railroad right-of-way
and a chain-fenced millyard.

There you were: naked,
your head a black glory richer
than the snakes of smoke from the steel mills
intertwining in the sky. For the first time
you saw yourself, I watched
the terrified unbelieving
opening of the eyes, and love that struggled
defeated from its birth.

NEAR RAVENNA

Just where the long white lake met the sand,
the slow motion of earth ruffled the weeds.
Sparse and thin, they swayed near under the surfaces
of viscid milky air and green water.

Which was more tired, the sky's watery pinks
and yellows, or your downcast face and voice,
your strengthless nervous fingers rummaging
in the shore's infinity of lucky stones?

And at day's end, the gentle powerful cold
that slips beneath taut skin and quiets frenzy,
uniting the vast spaces between adolescent thighs
to silent tracts of pine:
I know that you too felt its heavy passion
and surrendered.

THE GIFTS

The man and woman gave summer to be his alone,
an orange tree in blossom under a white brick wall
in the long street, a promise against thirst.
The towers, windows, and signs belonged to him too,
went with him, were heaped upon him
as he walked never ceasing to where the crowds thinned out.

At deserted crossings
music, wars, and all that they had done,
clank of keys, in the gusts thunder of tin,
the sky-blue scraps torn from plaster and blown
through the sun reddening a bare branch.

Immense, confused, among the cast metals, rusted,
in love he recalls, a face in agony carved in wood
under towering rock, by the snowy mountain path,
mouth torn open: make my word your home.

And the shattered
concrete of this empty street
must be illusion: there is no street, no pavement,
only the parents' footsteps – there's nothing here
but a step sounding past these images: failed nightclub,
arcade boarded up, wooden unpainted house, empty door.

He wanted to go inside
and as if in ignorance stare
blankly at half of a doll, a ledger, snapshot, cup,
all that is left there:
not one cracked letter left explaining,
not a shard of a sentence in a drawer.

But no need or reason to reenter what is mine.
Leaving they kept nothing, in these rooms
everything good and evil was given to me,
along the flat facades walks with me here.

Utterly shut up in the sound of wind around corners
of these orderly blocks, in dripping wires,
he wants to celebrate and knows he can.
Even cut off, what endless pleasure there is
in every moment, and how long it takes to die.

LE PARESSEUX

Naked – even his sunshade hat and his staff
he's laid aside to lie back on the soft young rocks,
and the pruning hook and scythe have dropped from his hand:
someone else will have to wield them, later.
But now the landscape ripens, dusk
spaces recessional to a glowing distance,
the feathered trees unknown to science,
a long aisle to a just-sunken sun.
In this, the latest light that is still intense,
somehow unburnt by the years of wandering
unclouded noons, he almost sleeps,
wrists hung among stems, fingertips in the grass-tips.

Distraction, the girl in coffee shops,
to her left a cheap clay pot of flowers,
the angry colours bursting in deep sleep,
ravished, against the flat conflicting background
of littered tabletops she's wiping, of chipped
crockery, moons and melon sections daubed
on curtains buckled, faded, by light and wind.

Here he can see a tree hang down its oranges
toward his unclosing hands, and stone steps,
long worn hollow, rising up the stony hill
to a small temple woven of saplings and thatched.
From it the fruit would be unseen under the leaf-crown.
Could not be reached or tasted with the eyes.
Would grow, sway, fall, unknown to anyone
who climbed and looked out in that frail house up there
for the storm, the night that so far never comes.

THE TRAVELLER

Once the sun used to rise every day,
in its light how feeble the man and woman became,
shouts were broken, doors opened
on flowering lilacs and the road.
A traveller who hates his destination, his one hope,
absorbed, walks quickly
with a loved memory he won't recall:
there never will be time. Just once
he falters between the river and his speed,
to dream of a vast thirst bringing insanity before death:
a girl who has as yet no breasts
but knows already how to strip and bathe
a wounded man, his wound that has made him safe,
spread open on the grass, for a child's curious approach.

Dark shining dawn. The creaking of this sufferer's
slow collapse frightens women in the next room:
homeless women, their houses burnt, collected sleeping here.
Their purple eyes, as if cut, as if beaten, open wide.
Crying, a long night slumped against a wall.
'Welcome, son. Though you left us and you are the one
who killed our men, we've made our bodies ready.'
Afternoon exhausts itself once more outside this house:
ready to be cut, ready to be planed and nailed,
the nervous trees age, darken and quiet down.

ENTRANCE TO TIVOLI

Look up: the broken half-circle
of pillars on the high rock in the distance,
and bright, human in glorious woods,
that room by the falling of roof and wall laid open.
Two crownless towers the green seizes on the deep hill.
And farther: the aqueduct collapsed in crossing the dark gorge –
calm power of endurance, that an arch still flies
white over that shining leaf-dark and blinding
sun on the black river.

These few ruins dispersed over the vast tract you see
relentlessly flowering: my city, or what remains.
To try to recall where the streets went,
the footsteps: only this effort now connects
the empty doorways that are still to be more empty.
If a shepherd and his sheep, surprised by the storm,
will huddle there between a squared rock toppled
by fire and a rounded rock
toppled by wind, then for one night again
the place has works, a government, a life.

Now it's time to leave you and go up there:
but watch, guard, clothe yourself while I'm gone.
Here night itself is warm, yes,
stone is soft, yet cover your sex and thigh
as you lie back to watch, to sleep.
Take this white cloth fringed with blue and red,
and hide your breasts too as long as it's day, even dusk:
as long as there's still light to shine on the sleeping rock
and on the blackness of deep green
that climbs at sunset from the gorge up to this lookout.

I'll go to Tivoli – a few days, no more,
will find me at the first black arch.
Here you'll be safe, and I'll bring you back some news.
And then the two of us will go up together,
if anything but shattered peace is still there.

3

City Plan

MORNING, LONELINESS DIED

Morning, loneliness died, dark heights and valley burnt
and you were there, sunlight on your darkened bricks.
From deepest ore the last of metal was disappearing:
engines – how uncertain they were, repetitive, I heard,
they stuttered, fell apart – dragged you without pause.

In white light someone opened a letter far away,
looked, threw it fluttering on the pile. Crowds
jammed through the passages, overfull.
Sweet with unreachable, unendurable sweetness,
a simple music – two notes, one time –
went on and on to crush your watery
returnings of the dead, never to leave you.

Joyous, impassive, you did not permit yourself a comment
on stone, steel, crane, drunkenness, window, star,
a dream of significance. And the hard wall of a woman's
afflicted skin, a man's laboured breathing and scabs,
might torture some, but you don't sanction any outcry. Wind
in a thin tree in the lee of your walls.
And where else is there? Rain. Your loud dead,
lapping, drowning each thought,
whispering under the tires.

CITY PLAN

1 Democracy, yet a king
  murdered his son
  for the foundation of the first wall:
  a legend. And we know it, my people,
  sunning ourselves, leaning against the bricks
  with a cold eye on black draped
  women rummaging through salted fish,
  bruised fruit
  with a cold eye.
  Deepening snow trampled into yellow mud.
  Calm self-mockery of the sun, sunken again
  into the stiff tangled nets of the vineyard,
  the dreary ruin
  of the brickyard. Our locked
  unpainted huts on the peripheries,
  white windows flowing
  with cataracts of frost.

2   Large flakes of cool skin, browning, fall
    from magnolias on the concrete
    path darkly curved through moist lawns,
    silent mansions. And as if a last
    cloth had been torn away, shredded,
    sifting to the ground, a boy,
    naked, a girl,
    runs past the houses, fearing to be seen, scented
    in vacant loveliness. Rain
    releases the bound perfumes:
    soil, beetles and worms
    struggling softly, crushed, and grasses, flowers.
    What should the defenceless one do,
    the violated, with virginity that has gathered again
    to rage in deserted day, untamable night?
    Fear, hope. But no door opens
    in gently burning tree, face, or wall,
    the spouse or the destroyer
    will not look out, is never tempted
    by the supple animal
    alone in the barren clearings.

3   Foreign and quiet are the nighttime walls
    of our houses, and the foaming wave
    that clears the ground. From surging crowds, distant
    shots, laughter, crystal lights
    subside and sink
    in this deep green. Our country, eternity,
    passing in a night for one who sleeps here
    or wakes. Remember the dead virgin,
    the boy, and a man who survived, whose talons once
    dreamed in a downy sweetness
    that he seized from earth and carried up to air.
    Now it is his alone, part of his flesh: so he still soars,
    rich in fruit, petals, leaves,
    over an empty tree. So, nailed to one another,
    in blue glowing blackness they glide away,
    among broken arms and rafters,
    in the forest cathedral. Youth.

4 Just as, newly torn
   out of childhood, a boy prays, 'How long
   until I start desiring death,
   Lord, so that this sun can burn
   into rich green voices, a memorable season,'
   this morning's bloodlike cloud turns white and gray.
   Mother, won't you ever pass,
   but always be there in mid-stagger
   in front of warped bare siding, cracked windows of old houses,
   leaning into that snow, in black,
   under the black spheres, cylinders, walls
   of the refinery? Just as, newly born
   in dirty straw, in the eye,
   in Toledo or Canton, a woman cries wonderingly
   over her infant, and her rifted face
   watches, mocks, nails her smooth young face,
   on this windy corner,
   old age and the storm bow your head.

ALONG THE RAILS

The portion, wandering,
the cruel and useless portion,
we took it for ourselves.

With the sunset I was waiting –
waiting: our word for to be and last and pass away –
waiting to explain, or be understood.

Along the rails between glass plant, brick plant, steel plant
and the dark banks, there grew and flowered the ideas,
science, medicine, song: sombre gold, deep green and flowing water.

Sometimes one configuration of cloud
and purple smoke, burning at day's end, or one perfectly blank sky,
seems to sum up a life, a city and a people.

The town crept on the earth, dripping
a dripping fire, clouds that sink in darkness, and always
new cars and old drove through its simple designs.

Who needs another thing? We are home –
the food plentiful, rust, the waiting earth
that keeps us busy, that buckles the concrete.

SECRECY

The boy was found naked, murdered
in the course of no one knew what shame, and they carried him
    into our house,
his red hand cupped on his genitals. Amazement:
my mother putting aside once her disgust
laid his head back in her arms and washed him gently
for burial. Tenderly washed every part of him.
This happened once. Why every day do you repeat it?

Your fingers were stumbling on the piano, stumbling in the waltz,
agèd footsteps, a presage of drunkenness.
Everyone in our family was old, our younger sister the oldest,
our family come from nowhere with no stories,
no skill, blank faces, only laws.

Stand again in the long gone iron swirling of leaves
under silver maples torn apart, glinting unconquered.
Thrash with your rake.
Heap dark gold mounds of leaves the wind deranges
under that white wall and brutal window,
bare end-of-autumn grass to the longed-for snow.

In the tearing, hissing air around this house,
if a calm hour comes, deep blue, dazzling,
it's rage worn out. The wrecked stone heads,
male and female, persist, always eroding
very slowly, by the bedroom's broken door.

So writing an endless letter of your anger
never set down. So many august feelings:
would a century be enough to give form to even one?
And then the rest would have breathed themselves away
with the slow gray river, the mists, the fireflies
rising among these houses in that just-ended summer.

OUR SISTER

Our sister came out into the garden, more beautiful than ever,
still littered with debris from the forgotten storm,
hands, groins and heads cracked from statues and trees.

Was there anything we wanted from her anymore? The power
of stillness was complete and final, the dark ditch and hedges,
the oak, owl, star, cloud, possessed it in simplicity.

In that hour just before birds wake, even the anger
of the childbed wasn't yet singing: the one movement there,
our sister, walking naked, intending nothing, a naked hour.

Then she sat on a toppled marble bench, clothed by the love
of her legs closed as if in sleep, by the shell, her hand,
laid open as though broken, forgotten, in her lap.

Thus dressed for the street in cheap ill-assorted clothes
miming the fashion she went out. To us through the blind came
many figures of a great yellow horn, headache's empire.

The farther away your beauty is, the higher it seems.
The gray cracks that once spread across it, locked in your room,
are like this new moment, our need for you pondered, lost.

In the long light we have sometimes burst out: Sister,
come back. But why? Your soft decline imitates a girl alone,
and many grow strong desiring you so, always young.

STOPLIGHTS

In the failing chatter of young women,
fascinating: her pleasure in the silver falling water,
white trees and tables, and a meek boy now curves,
gentle, setting down a glass of water.

Space fills with agèd women, unseen, unheard,
the century's best loved songs, an old belief,
dusk hasn't come. Rose, then, the shadow:
from withered necks, a gray grid: streets, night, belief.

In the fields beyond town, red horses doze.
A doctor, thick and stiff, blunders in the holy pictures
in a dead girl's room. She sat here many years,
her bronze face ever sharper in the pictures:

a naked rider trying to feel skin, saddle, death.
Welcome rest, to float, dissolve, and this low mutter,
soft night that fear makes harsh: her car drives,
stoplights halt her at crossings, gray windows mutter.

FRESH GRAVE

The dead child who passed through here centuries ago
was looking for something ancient,
something close enough to endlessness to be worthy of song.

Maybe a bound sheaf of wheat and a sickle
such as are minted on coins, but standing in a field
and not simple gold or silver: the colour of dying fire,
the colour of bread, of an old tool covered with earth and rain.

She went by herself and she was angry that couples
and small laughing groups dithered by unkept walls,
or in the long path under the high tension lines,
or along abandoned sidings – anywhere winter had made
a brown, hard, clicking, glinting garden
of dried goldenrod, bricks, twisted wire, and thistles.

How many centuries has she been dead? She walked
a whole life long without ever coming to an end
of our neighbours, our streets and houses, this gray sky.
Set out after her and long before you reach the outskirts,
if there are any outskirts, you'll find her fresh grave,
her carved memorial stone and struggling tree.

OMNISCIENCE

Remote, serious, the dead sister and dead father wait.
Their human weaknesses have fled,
now they know everything and are absolutely silent.

Stillness: the peace and torture of ancient images.
There is no knowing of everything, though pleasure is still painted
in blue contemplation in ruins under wooded hills.

But the dead father and sister are perfected and austere.
Under their mute comprehension the one left behind,
a naked youth, disintegrates, eating his wrinkled eyes.

ON A SCREEN

Child of an assassinated country,
an assassinated hope – that all the fruits
of the long never maturing struggle,
the one that twists, cuts, burns the limbs
from men and women, centuries of sweet
desiring limbs dropping in the pail...
those fruits would erupt at last from a new, mild
contention of brothers, of sisters. Belovèd,
follow our sirens to thread the million characters
of your fear, weaving your way
as fancifully as the forest of right angles
permits, the office towers more populous
than the great towns of your childhood were,
airy dungeons of virgins, female and male,
violated. The million answerers
from a million wells are one answer from a dark
space, a depthless earth:
no need, then, to be confused.
You will be different, one day, if you endure.
There's a promise of it even in your nights,
if you consent to know them: blank pleasure,
suffering: you lie down
and are nothing – a television screen,
not even a thought or a seeing, but the unseen
images of this worldwide helpless day
that are flowing in your body, are taking your form.

WAITING FOR A PARADE

Murmur of the poor behind your back:
bagging the garbage littered over the plain.
Mopping. A pinched voice whines to her friend
drowned in fats. Sometimes they pick out
a useful or affecting object from crumbled kitchens:
a broken clock, blocks of the dead child, their sister.

What is far away is beautiful: wealth,
the unimagined. They want ice, time, death to live.

Fired again. Fired with the confusions
of your purpose upon you, and set adrift again in these streets.
So a monk drifts in the square
monastery garden, the white baking wall,
the cross of the paths cutting four zones in the earth,
each with its one tall withered emblematic plant
bowing, swaying, dropping dust like a tower.

The wooded ridges and the stream have been made straight.
In this wine obscure in green bottles, cradle yourself
as in a salt-thick sea – and on broken glass, on the concrete.
This is where it will inevitably pass.
Wait, you've already waited till the end,
murmur of the poor behind your back.

4

Founders

VISIT HOME

Returning, I saw that land still burnt
under the highway's lash – more than ever. And driving on,
I saw it burning now too from the sun.
That August the branches joined the motors
in rattling empty shells together.

Mahoning's land: its flesh was cracking open
and falling away, blowing in yellow grass and disappearing:
the white sky and low river had withdrawn their water.

Winds mocked the dryness with an idle stir,
a flowing hush over brittle leaves and the sand:
water music, and the creek was
a marsh of brown blood drying in a damp bed.

Crowded along a thousand brittle arms with skin
mummified on the bones (arms, dry branches
that clashed in the wind and broke each other), locusts

were singing. That August, over everyone
who entered its cities, the land held
dripping from gray wrists
the fog-like webs of the tent caterpillar.

*

Dying summer was powerful and greedy
around fence posts, in ditches and vacant lots.

Vengeful summer, unbroken:
calm, the destroyer put its hand
to crumbling edges of the streets.
The invisible fire
that rose out of tar,
out of asphalt and brick
and shook the air and sucked blood,
turning leaves to shells

and mummified hands
and living skin to paper –
that was her anger.

*

In that August of granite-coloured haze, Mahoning's land
was like a burning ash about to crumple
while it still holds the shape of the leaf it was.

Dry blue showed faintly through the rock-red air.
The slopes and fields and lots were powder:
a human hand
could sift them,

could search for that land in the ash of its own body.
Where was it: under slag and ore between the ties,
among baking lucky stones
bared by the lake's retreat, below the old waterline?

Burnt, dried out, crumbled,
it would not let me remember how to love it.
Almost asleep, I twisted in the night about to break
in flames, and reached to touch its neck
and it whispered: Not until
my water returns to me.

But it seemed an ocean of sweet water
was dispersed above us, almost ours: at night
it sweat on our dry ribs and cried
in the silent strain of trying to exist once more.

*

It seemed that Mahoning was preferring its own death,
that I saw it struggling to forget the other

that had been brought to it: all the muzzles
of cattle and the human snouts
lined up at its veins: titanic herds
poured out of black steel barns,
fouling the stream below the sea-green hay,
there, where three oaks lean out from the bank.

There water eats at yellow clay and undermines the fisted roots.
In shade the white seeds winding down are a memory
of what nothing remembers: unseen, the wet arched darkness
that once was here, its kindly light
and cool paths. I used to think of it
as the interior of a happy body: rich black labyrinth
as of lungs and a throat beneath a calm, closed mouth.

But could I, by the drying river and land,
prefer ancient, unknown summers:
unknown, or rarely glimpsed by the early people,
who in twos and threes had passed swiftly, hunting
the beaver, their own god? Could I prefer
the forest fire, lost glory of unpeopled August,
to reservoirs feeding the sea of grain?
Prefer that mouth of ashes
where the lightning once destroyed
the fleeing deer's household –
prefer that power to our smoke
that rises even out of snow, our phalanxed
blazing intent on the eternal
behind the blast furnace door?

FIRST

At earliest morning
before the fog
falls, crumbling, tearing
to shreds, to droplets,
from beneath my willow
in my parents' yard I watched
the first lonely worker's arms
swing at his sides: the lighted
haze turned them to black wings, mighty,
milling above the pavement. He went by
to the Republic Works. Then the sun
came slowly along
the sidewalks from the east,
from the creek, pouring under the lowest
branches when dew brightened
on the lawns, the first
dog barked, tethered
among sunflowers, the ways filled
with men on their way
to the mill, and a gold and black
garden spider moved
scattering silver, to test
her cold web.

My nape purring
at light's touch, my fingers
already stained with following
the track of the ant, eager,
unable to wait longer, I was
a call to your sleeping children.
As the dawn wind
softened and warmed, mine was the first
cry that echoed between houses,
the first knock on your door.

EAST WALL

The first thing: learned under the east wall of the house
in April. Early morning. It's good to be here.
Black confusion still sparkles in the rooms left behind,
here the moist soft fire of lilac, the same quiet sun
flows in the cat's fur and the child's hair.

It's good to walk under the shining wall,
its blinded windows. All stabbing sharpness died long ago
from gold, from brilliance, a long unimagined psalm
floated in the sleepers' eyes, mangled and shrouded.
This sun will rise still higher, these diamond-bearing
maples will burn, the teachers open the door
and walk into a brown day.

The boy runs to the stream bank: one discipline
to which he can submit. On mirroring water
all houses waver, doors flicker among trees,
broken branches, ends of streets, windows, seeds and leaves
drift southward. Distant words walking on the current,
dusty, as though wishing to sink, have passed nearby.
Good will: these are my mother, my sisters and my brothers,
with wood and sky, pure, in darkly shining water.

SHADE

Vines, dark-lacquered, each broad leaf
holding out its fragment sun,
cover the wall of red brick
and beard the silent
open windows. And are trembling
with hidden wrens, their trills,
thrashings, squabbles
and sometimes a violent, quick
parabola of one
out to the peach tree, back
into shadow.

The sun gives itself also
on the blades of the blue-green
pine needles – sharp, thin,
they could stab through
a child's black pupil
with their sun-tips: so we were careful,
full of fear, and went slow,
when we would crawl to rest
in the pine's dark – to lie there
on the brown, scented
bed that the fallen
needles made, soft as our own hair.

Loved hour of coolness, pause
sunk, a well, into memory,
what were you – that you changed,
ebbing away, like the glistening
day beyond you, the vibrating
glory we spied on from your shade?
And soon we would leave
that shelter, adventure again
where now the inhuman power
that sucks colour remorselessly
from flower and leaf
was making nightfall.

Before it comes, we'll go
in under the tulip tree where even
the low slanting western light
can't reach us – we'll kneel on black
stones edging the pond
to harry red fish
circling among lilies. A slow
freight train passes: at that calm,
monotonous, belovèd music we look up
to the railroad embankment
that rises just beyond our fence,
then farther to the mill's
smoke, glowing
in a sky of fiery rust.

ONE WITH THE SUN

Child
one with the sun
in trackless fields
of yellow grass and thistle, scent
of humid heavy air and the wing music
of bees and flies.

Child, slender
nakedness to itself unknown,
true colour of the light
dispersed invisibly
or glowing around the black hulls
of distant thunderheads, around
the grasshopper's countenance,
solemn, vigilant and wise.

Green apples, poured full
of density, of crispness, float unmoved
under leaves on the slope. Brown
fallen apples nest
in secret whorls of grass. The apple tree:
alone in so much space. And below
in the woods by the water
a sweet dead branch
cracks lightly
in the shadow in the wind.

But here is an old track
through the grass head-high
to a child: who
made it? They must have
passed and passed by this one tree,
by the abandoned, tireless car
where rabbits peer out, and the circle
of black embers,
cans, springs, skeletons
of furniture. They too

passed here many times
on their way from the street's end
to the oaks that screen
the river. There
the sun is nesting now, night
rises with pale flutterings
of white wings from roots
of plants and the black water.

KINGDOM AND LEAVES

Kingdom and leaves: a child joined
these things together. The kingdom of leaves
runs from the low branches in your hands
up to the sky. And you can go up there,
climbing the branches, and rest inside that world.

The chimneys, balconies and roofs belong to it
and it belongs to the sparrows. They are the children there.
As if on lawns among gardens, hedges and houses,
they veer in their ragged crowds through secret shortcuts.
Pleasure is a maze found out in the summer dusk.

And there is always one flying far behind
all the others, who never stop. Kingdom of evening,
coloured like branches collapsing in a fire.
Crimsons pour from ash-blue clouds,
which wait now, and new cool distances,
new, humid lights appear – from how high up
and how far away sleep comes!

EVENING

Huge evening, calm, surging
fresh in the oaks, their green
darkness thrust up
swaying to touch steel-blue
and molten-iron colours fleeing higher
into blackness. Two brothers and a sister
swam in that newly absent
sun: its light,
its spectrum, deepest when dying,
flowed through the linked lawns
down tree-banked streets, swirling
quietly around the brick
and wooden walls.

Then orange windows
and white stars came out,
and their parents' eyes
watching calmly, far-off,
the children race amid
lightning bugs densest
in the dark under maple trees. Water
and sleep were gathering
where leaves cupped the slender
bases of the stems.

Did knowledge gather, too,
of what is to come, in tired sadness,
that those three children always hated
and refused sleep? But sleep
grows strong, its moist hand
indistinguishable from tears
brushes the young brow,
closes the eyes, and their sight
grows indistinguishable
from not knowing.

And the lawns with their now buried
trees and flowers rushed onward,
a never-varying pace
through unpeopled night, as if
stone-still in that plunge. Distant,
the long slow freight trains barely
shook the earth, the house,
the beds and the three
sleeping bodies. They stirred,
almost woke, felt the machine vibration
through the ground, in the walls,
as a nervousness of their own,
a dread: of what?

While the parents, the guardians,
awake beneath them in
the speed of the night, still saw
smokestacks thrust up
over houses and trees, saw smoke billows
whitened by moon and city light.
As the train crept
from the millyard, they heard
knowingly a distant sound
that stirred childish sleep again:
huge metal doors
heaved shut.

CENTURIES AGO

Worn voices were whispering amounts
in the next room and sometimes would cry out
or a body – perhaps a forehead – would sound sullenly,
muffled, against a wall. Mute noises: anger? Sobbing?
Impure mixtures, the voices, blows, the rainy wind, empty
flat-bed trucks clanking their chains under the silver maple tree
that night, slow crushing of concrete and black grass.

Summer dawns in your room, child: sunlight and living air
trembled in white curtains and threw them off.
Your body, self-revealed, naked to invisibility,
standing at the window still. And there is the archaic
word of prayer,
Thou Lord, scrawled below in burning dew,
and carved in the bark of a pine – those voices,
hands once, planted it centuries ago
to commemorate your birth.

FOUNDERS

Beautiful in its distance
the day burning down and flight of stars,
quiet in your eyes, disaster so far away
it is still forgotten music, ancient peace.

Incomparable, this human world: the vast
plain of black roofs,
light and music at the quiet crossing where five streets join.
Full of joyous prophecy is the flight of heraldic sparrows
in shifting rivers, childish, self-willed
flocks unravelling among elms at dusk. Women decay,
and houses stand open, orange light
streams from the torn eyes and mouths. Others are dark
as though ruined, abandoned last century
or this afternoon: in the distant day of the founders.

Hidden in a moist culvert with booming frogs,
tracks gleam bronze in the low sun and cattails
flow with white molten flax congealing.
Dusky slag. Purple thistle. Empty flowering fields,
guardian lights and chain-link fence. Decades, rust
made lace of black factory hangars on the river flats
and the red west burns through: pattern and quiet glory,
steel decomposing, new fire.

In the park a boy and girl stopped under oaks
and revolved the names: of the city, its streets, this park,
the long dead owners' names, their races
sunk in quiet shadow, fireflies and empty streets,
this black paving or ground.

Shouts of children, dwarfed
in the vast pleasure of coming night.
Arc, fall, thud, splash of balls and swimmers' bodies.
Evening, the eyes, the coolness of young skin
shining near water: such evening was your temple,

temple of pure distance, stones crumbled to their vacant form.
It was you glimmering, you the statue there.
Men in troops passed in through high burning metal doors,
hammers the strength of a thousand could never lift
fell in order, they felt that thumping in the ground
in their frames, a surer heart.

And here you were faintly smiling, not forgotten,
impassive, choked with prayers, worn by hands.
It was you who gave yourself up, your brow painted
with stars and massifs of cloud, your dance and voice
of frog and snake, cricket and locust, your age
more ancient, younger than the naked August night.

Gave yourself up without a cry, with your memories
of a people from far away, strange minds that built this place:
some were stunned at the fading, the mercy,
the strengthlessness of your memories.
The whole injustice of the earth – isn't it here? –
the whole failure of the blessing, in this wooden calm
of faces, walls, obscure
spaces, passion, peace. Too happy
for oracles, a father's or a mother's voice
mixed with gray slime and mist where childhood's stream
bleeds from the ground, you still were blessed with peace
by the one unknown.

THE UPPER STORIES

Overnight the house withered. Nothing was left
but a network of brittle planks hammered together
as narrow bridges tottering toward the sun,
and risen in joy and fear, the one asleep ran upward.
First in calm anxiety the leaves blazed and shook,
then clouds were all around, their gnawing moisture,
their pure speed over the fallen roof, the dark
furnace in its shattered basement, the brick and metal
pyramids, delicate, along a silver thread in a wood.

Now in autumn, deep gray and gold,
you can walk back under the harmless walls,
marvelling at the agèd weakness of your anger,
unpainted boards, apples mummified in overgrown grass,
some years an old woman opens a door
or a light goes on briefly in an upper room.

Elsewhere you live
and there are footfalls, fire, water under leaves
beneath a bricked-up room erect with many others.
The sun there reddens equal doorways endlessly,
a quiet light, a motor, dies,
and beauty is to walk there as long as can be
step by step with the curious one who never turns aside.

Freedom is that autumn street
in the outspread city, never vast enough,
astir with glinting darkness. As he passes, his tired head
slumps forward beneath each window, red or black.

5

The Faithful One

I

When we came awake, children in the meagre town
that shows so rich, deep, quiet, painted here,
already earth was becoming vision, becoming paint
spread over a vision to make it seen.

Children at the age of earliest memories:
one morning we found a sparrow newly dead
twisted in the warm tenderness of its feathers,
soft, light and dry, folded in its wings and our hands.
A bird flew past us – a daub of light – when we
turned over a crumbling log and saw the earwigs swarm,
felt the moist breaking, breathed perfume of deep decay.

Was it I who played naked like a painted god
with my sister by the stream? The way there
led far from home, down past the backs of things,
brick buildings, metal doors rusted shut for years,
black gaps glowing in mossy walls,
broken stairs of wood or stone. And then

a jay's tearing cry over the water full of dark dust,
blinding August soothed by trees with gold blood.
I've shown that day as it was: you seem to hear
the unseen locusts sing to the naked children,
permitting them everything. You smell
the dry coolness in the empty husk
of a factory that decayed in flowering weeds across the stream.

II

For years now those children have been gone
from these shadowy rooms and lawns,
flowers gleaming dead or living on their beds.
Many pure empty years have flowed around the house,
until stream and lake, woods, mirrors, are full of silver calm.

And I'm still living: should anyone live this long,
staring like this at house and grass and sky,
passing for a man but studying inwardly
to reach again, after years of rigid labour and determination,
what childhood was? Should anyone keep living
to paint a blank wall, the outward
skin of those days, as if calling out something within?

I wanted to draw from my studies of this house
clean lines of a sketchy wonder, or wonder dimly recalled.
But you only see, in the empty black windows and door,
vague shapes: hard, sharpened, full of care,
yet soft, soft as though rotting, if you could touch them:
the owners, the ones who grew up, inherited, and live there,
brothers and sisters still with me, whom I know well.

III

Frightening, the images that seem the very first:
not truly of a new world, if you look closely,
but a young world newly dead, already browning and twisted.

Here are the children, brother and sister, strictly recalled,
just as if ancient gods had posed for them:
they pause naked together, ankle deep in blue water,
in sex and limbs and green shadows the cold
unmoved depth of childhood, on leaves and flesh the light.
And the frame of the campagna grew around them: shattered
masonry, willows, sunset.

Will I ever learn to be sorry for what I've loved,
to let that twilight go, let it die in this night?
Will I ever learn to repent what I once loved?
Easier to mix colours than atonement and celebration,
easier to confuse forms. Though an old man,
I turn with disgust from my disgust,
turn each day on the gray bed, get up, draw them again
naked, impassive, without care ...

A painter of shadows and the waves of salt.
But the heart of that summer was my heart.
Behind this paint, laid bare:
how still in the dead room I cherish and repeat my pleasure,
to fall and rise, each day, to rise and fall.

IV

Instead of the empty house where they truly lived
under winglike eaves and the wings of mother and father,
here I show those children as I dream them now,
wanderers. The elder brother
shepherds the still smaller pair through a black street.
Already he knows himself: the guardian.
For him there is to be no forgetting of the law,
no flight from his charge,
never any mistaking how little can be done.
Never will he blindly, deeply love an illusion
and so be forgiven. No messenger
will appear in his dark and command him to violate.
To err in innocence will belong to others.

You are to understand his stonelike head
as longing for the blessèd hour of emptiness.
Though you may laugh
at the archaic ring of the laws, you are to hear him
as repeating inwardly: it is not allowed
to go mad, forget everything,
sin with the sister – not allowed.

V

Or I showed the ancient hero, young,
with massive sword- or cross-like staff in hand,
returning through the steep valley along chrome sheets of water,
broken towers on ridges, a fallen aqueduct,
no one. (There,
where I gave birth to myself,
was only the tying of a knot
of self-love in the sun and the river –
the river that ran on, giving no sign,
filling its tortuous course with the same
uninterrupted peace.)

And I placed, approaching the striding hero,
a young woman or man in a red robe who gestures madly
into the deep glowing cleft: the words
are lost in distance. O scent of willow bark
I dreamed to capture, fresh water between reeds and stones,
a dragonfly's whisper, and the human cry:
round and hollow, as if to far-distant death;
agonized but low, secretly joyous,
as if fearing death might come;
an actor's cry, longing for an end
and to repeat itself.

The time is near darkness. Fireflies
in the grass-tips. Hush of a distant
highway all night long, and the slamming,
once, far off, of giant metal doors. Painting I heard,
and you can still hear, the descant of three locusts.
A rusting tractor, because the scene is not all ancient,
our world intrudes: also, a huge blank sign
held up above unworked fields on a steel pillar.
Here and there in the depopulated woods
a roof shows through the leaves,
or the conveyor of an abandoned gravel pit.

VI

Wonder: now I have wife and children of my own,
and my eldest son is a father to the young ones.
My eldest son – a better head for business than mine ever was.
He organizes the students and disciples
to fill in backgrounds and complete minor commissions:
we have a regular factory, are growing rich.

Wonder: in the last century, when the others
all had to have their schools, workshops and assistants,
I was original – a solitary genius, the first,
just out of ignorant stubbornness and poverty
and the loved memories that ate at me.
And now that the modern century's come
and they're all solitary geniuses together,
it's I alone who know the beauty of a common style,
clear, long familiar, well loved, reproducible by many
but supple, and with the capacity to bear great weight
when – rarely, rarely – a great weight comes.

And my son will be the master of this style.
As he is more practical and hard,
so he has greater depths, more gentleness than I have,
intenser love and calm. How much this new style will say,
how usefully, and still with how much silence.
I wish I could fall down and love this son of mine,
stop, fall down, hold, only love him
and paint no more, be satisfied.

VII

An ancient village: cringing animals snarled, fought, were killed.
Walls of mud. They cut their food with shells,
down a stinking alley the thin girl drove her younger sisters,
homeless already, setting out to find the shepherd's hut.

Later her child, about the size and shape of a young toad smashed,
was held out for me to view on a trowel blade, stainless steel,
the sort used here to delve gravel and smooth blue oil.

Those old men were rich and strong, why did you go with them?
Were we fearful, absent, thin, dead, faithless,
one with them: why did you go?

She answered: I dreamed I was alone,
nothing I could do was ever to be seen or wanted,
there was howling everywhere
and I could rest at last.

A voice: not to be drawn, described, captured,
and so, though it existed, merged with all the rest.
Her naked back turned, she bathed
with her sisters once at the stream bank
one quiet hour, unknowable among the others,
so many beauties, flesh laid bare, in the soft reaping light.

VIII

A stair up into hawthorn scent and dense magnolia,
where light spreads from within, from white globes glowing.
Also from within there, a woman's sound: crying
and choking, suppressed, timid, without end.

Everywhere in the perfumed night, burnt oil, lilacs,
in leaning doorways, lit windows, down alleys, under these trees,
the desperate voice shrieking protest or, humble, sobbing.
The sound of motors sometimes covers it –

and if they quiet, maybe it has died away, worn out,
or moved on to where it can't be heard. Later, walking,
nervous, someone looking even in this night
for calm, a place where there's no one, turns down

between two high brick walls, blank, cracked mortar and lintels,
a hissing bulb ... and it meets him there: a voice –
as if the Madonna of Bellini spoke – obscene,
a muffled screech, cursing, begging, hoarse with frustration.

IX

Cleopatra dies, Tabitha is raised
in the same vast room, higher than any sky,
darker, thicker, more swarming than black earth.
Instead of heaven, purple silk like blood drying in folds.
For mountains and clouds: hands and weapons confused,
lost architecture, stairs and arches up into resinous dark.

But the creator of these scenes was no Antony, no Peter,
only a shivering mouse who saw it all from under the floor,
a shivering boy, unobserved, who saw it – saw what they did.

By heroic labour – standing at the canvas more grimly than a rock,
more joyfully than a spray-ruined foam-crowned rock
that glitters in pounding sun – turning my sole eye
to the conception carved within me,
I would see that we live right: all pain ours,
yet in the Grecian bodies that weigh so lightly.

Look: you can see in the brown-black oil of the deepest recess
one eye horrified and staring. Here light gleams on daggers,
on a war-sandalled foot and ankle like an oak trunk –
listen: clanking of arms, shouts, moans, trumpets.

And in this one, wailing. The wailing deafens me,
sickens me, clogs my throat, crushes my temples –
the screaming around green Tabitha
as the old saint, uncertain, stooping, bald, approaches slowly,
one arm half raised in a weak, aging gesture.
Vast now, he totters over me – once so small in my mind's eye.

X

I had an assistant, a boy deaf and dumb from birth,
who would sit all day sadly in a corner of the studio,
and in the evenings sit sadly by my wife.
I remember him crouching, huddled on the floor,
watching, as the one who had lain there in front of me,
naked a moment ago, came back, now dressed for the theatre.
Not glancing at herself on the canvas, she screeched,
'Are you finished, won't you ever
be finished?' and I threw her down.
A curious bacchante. Servile. Greedy.
Unremitting. She shows to advantage in this nude,
her nether hair more gently curled and parted
by nature than her mane has been by art,
and so in truth it was. As she wanted, she's rich now.
Dark, the fearful head, her eyes blacker
and flatter than the ribbon round her throat,
yet deep. That despairing intelligence offered this body up
to love, to save itself. On the head I've printed clearly,
as in pure Castilian, the childish stratagems:
it thinks how to dispose the limbs and so make its way.
And on the body, perfect, this childlike expression.
The two know nothing about each other's dream,
body and head: are proud and uncomprehending of each other,
each has the other in its gift and betrays.
Which is the unworthy one,
which one is most harried, merciless, unsubjugated?

An image immortal in a burnt-out flash of the eye,
one to rouse a man, sicken him, and make him strong.
But I crouch in a corner staring, and can't find
why we desire them, what we hoped for,
and my own life, the touch of life, in endless looking.

XI

The car drove us hurriedly all night,
we passed the border safely, and afterwards,
this is how we looked – I gouged the scene then
on a rag of paper with charcoal from the cold grate:
how we looked, my aging wife and I,
alone in that miserable room for the first time.
Sometimes in my sleep there I heard my mother again
shouting for me to come in, angrily, worried:
my childhood name – maybe it was Paco, William,
or Albrecht. And I felt anxiety again
as if for the first time – I felt the adult command
intrude under those bushes by the stream
where the girl and I had laid our clothes aside.
How immense and quiet
is the gray sky here, the blank wall. Old age.

Near the end, and still laying on too much colour.
Try to be honest: this is no divine madness, only exile.
Simply, the party we favoured and worked for failed;
another came to power. This is an ordinary thing,
poverty in old age, just as I expected it.
Carefully nurturing obsessions is not madness.
To invent and portray a madness is not to be released,
not even while the deep look and the portrayal last.

I'll dominate these phantoms – I'll
attain the sad lucidity
that melds the mind, the forms, the style,
to harrow all the hells we see,
then fall into that ground, and die ... O love,
why do I still fly to what may come,
a god come to us, a god we may become,
when the whole earth is thick with what we are?

XII

I wanted to have visions and see only at the end
you, love – how I squandered you,
forgot you while you were beside me,
even in your birth agony,
even when you were handing me my gifts.

Receptacle of an unfelt life. Now you alone
live and move here, draw your shape on the air,
torture and bring me back myself.
Your face: the strange beauty,
gentleness that made nonsense of the world.
You, shoved aside, watching attentively,
sometimes in admiration, sometimes crying,
how in yourself did you save
all that was thrown away or passed by?

I'm sick of silent images. Even these of your face
shown as it is: with blue earth and streams and air
stretching out humbly, servant-like, beneath you.
You will be dead, dead silence of memory and art
will swallow your voice, your hand. I'm sick
of fading, sick of silent images, come nearer, talk,
touch me, pure form
violated by all things
and mine alone, unportrayable, my love.

XIII

Ancient relentless pourings of the cricket
sank in our hearts, children
in that exhausted town,
to the heart of the dry crumbling loam –
moisture of late summer nights, when the ripe peach
hangs spectrally. You come again,
refreshed you come forward,
no longer overawed as when wild eagerness in me
would only loose the reins –
and you, dazed, white and small,
and the cruel noon,
hooves pounding
a fiery drum of sand and spray.
Now darker joy falls
and I recognize you, hear you cry,
your breasts weigh with sun and moon at dusk,
now darker joy
falls, empty.

XIV

I dreamed I wanted
as in the beginning this world always new:
change always. But change itself was the dead
unvarying sameness of things. A sensitive wire,
I registered each acceleration of the corpse
and at the end saw this:

a young wife calms the dark receding rooms.
I see her going around naked in our house,
green curtains drawn against remorseless August.
Or she sits, her winglike hands folded on her pen.

In the rhythmic confusion of your hair: my sun.

Unknowable, what you carry in your eyes:
fear, love, as if stones ripened. At the roadside
you were crying with one of your dead,
in the widening desert of the motors' noise
drinking the silence of God. Around you that steel,
those streets, that scrub, still harrying you, won calm.

The night fills with passersby and empties.
Who knows that you're here with me in the house?
And the dead sister and brother bringing you their green
dust-shrouded stream under maples and blue-forged sky:
sorrow, that we alone still meet them
playing naked by your restless voice once more.

XV

Beautiful women. Heroic actions. Disasters,
death. Ghosts. Melted faces. Stars.
The inner night. Landscapes quit interesting me.
And yet I would always paint the grass:
common, endless leaves, each one
distinguished by love. I came to think of the blank –
wall, canvas, frame – as the gift of madness:
how to cover it, suffering?
I remember seeing a face whose mouth was only a slash,
stretched, twisted, and I slashed it in charcoal
and bloodlike umber on a white page.
Then that black face that came from night
took me up in its hand, bit off my head, drooling blood:
and it came to be my new head, sole in triumph.

And yet I saw that one day it won't be needed:
there will be no more need of angry images,
tortured ghosts, women on the cross,
shots at night in the dark
collapsing pit of the Insurrection, the noose
hanging from clouds, captives slumped against a wall,
no more of this blinded noise, no need
to make people turn to me, no need
of horror. Only an unknown
calm, rising colours, red and blue, green, gold
and white, in the blackness. Absorbing love,
the heart of each thing, floating, free, even pain,
pain unto death,
unto suicide. A new art.

6

Following The Mahoning

GIVEN

Hills softened and borne down
under the glare. Tired,
the wind comes through the dense
air, dragging
a trail over rattling corn.
Before the green wall, panting,
a rabbit can hear
the sun: a roar, faint, from far
beyond the dragonflies' tangle.

Here out of morning haze
comes the river and shines,
earthen. But in the low
places between fields, its curtain
of trees is drawn: lone
blades, elegant – wild
timothy, wild wheat –
bow by the bank in shaded
hollows. Who here once drank
the reluctant dark, and joined
the gnats' hymn, saw the amber
breathing of jewelweed flowers
suspended under leaves?

You stood above the water
under the bridge, narrow,
old iron, that crosses the river. Empty
hour after hour, its tar
and asphalt vault above,
drink heat, choke, crepitate.
Anger and thirst. The water slides
under, against green stanchions,
away.

Beached on a low island
of three sycamores, the huge
tire of a truck, split open,
glowed, its body blacker than the black
shadows, and blackest was the dark inside
its wound. One tree
had fallen there long ago
and under the arch of its shattered
trunk a muskrat left her sign,
her track of stars in the cool mud.

IN NILES

City threaded
on bronze or iron-green
tracks and rivers. Overshadowed
by maples and the oak forest,
a remnant, on steep
ridges – boughs stir
over black roofs and a window
streaming light: dusk,
a child's foot crushes leaves
at the long-abandoned quarry's edge.

A road unwinds
out of the gutted wood,
on its rusted bridge it crosses
Mahoning, veiled
by sycamore and ailanthus.
From a weedy slope the houses
lean: splintered sill, door open on thick heat,
a boy in gray who looks down
to water flashing rarely
beyond leaves. And farther,
above trees on the opposite bank, a brick
mass, a high white stack
and black aqueduct: the power
plant in the crook of the unseen river's
resting arm.

Still clouded with mosquitos
where no one goes, behind
gravel lots
the bank sounds:
the plop of frogs, a wing sweep.
Streets, twisting and cracking, sidewalks, houses
turn their backs and
climb away from there.

You left them and came along
the railroad embankment, ditches
where milkweed lifts
its swollen sacks. Mating
dragonflies moor to dark
ironweed flowers, a flying grasshopper –
who hid among ties, woodchips,
pellets of ore
the hopper cars had flung – now

opens a gold black-banded wing
suddenly, sails, is gone. Crossings,
rusted sidings, switches, long
parallels through the scrub.

And you learned this way alone,
a child, behind the distant backs
of the buildings. Crossed the river, saw
old, rotted wooden stairs
that climbed down to the water
from locked forgotten doors. Found
a stove-in boat, a clay path
grown over, leading up beside the bridge.

Anxiousness and peace, vast,
the violet sky, a trudging step
toward night. The blackbirds
arced, paused
in tall weeds and mourning doves
were talking by the wall
of the empty factory,
black wall, unending grid of broken
windows: it is always
cool here, dark,
ancient dust, ancient metal –
we're at home.

FACTORY SHELL

Here, this beaten iron, this steel shed
in the river meadow, this black hangar
empty, where you could sleep –
night is inside though the thistle
flares, purple, in white light
against the wall.

Over there, across the flowering
deserted field and crumbling street
are the houses, wooden, unpainted. The sun
breaks on yellowed peaks,
on a vacant doorframe, a tethered
sheet that streams out and sweetens
on the wind. But here: the corroded metal
houses of this giant town, by the ragged
bank, mosquito-hung, the rusted tracks, in brush
crossed by one faint children's path.
Some are partly fallen:
steel plates and beams
sown in the ground.

Here a high black doorway calls
for a human body, much vaster than your own.
The shadow there:
if your thought had a thousand
bodies you might wake it, settle it
and make it work again. But now your dwarfed
shape, darkened, your sombre ears recall
eyes, mouths turned
to a hoarse furnace,
the unrecollected breath
of the newcomers: once
they moved darkly here, red faces
blazing, eagerness annealed
in the haze of the pickling mill.

A PRAISE

1 To sing
an earth delved but unknown, cities
as they rose left
falling into the ground ...
to magnify a fullness
of pleasure held out on every hand
and never taken ... to praise, here,
your first song used to yearn and reach
to twilit fields of young wheat,
the streams that pass between
leaf borders secretly
and under the roads.

And a remnant
of ancient forest shaded the naked song:
agèd now, but it still wants
to lash out and still is soothed by the love
it bears from childhood: for the rails
and roads thrust
through Mahoning's land, the bleeding streams
and ridges, gold
and water-coloured valleys,
the flowering swamps,
tatters of maple and oak.

2 On the roads always
cutting into that deep
braided world, bright or cloud-troubled,
driving, you drank awe.
You wondered at the lonely open doors,
shadow within, and windows
that flashed on empty fields
at noon in the dark
of willow and cedar. The light stood
swarming with odours: hay,
the grass and tiger lily of ditches,

clover by white houses
and barns, red
or paintless and collapsed. A foal

played on the far blue bank,
you touched the cows' strange rest
at the wire fence in the oak shade.
The mustard was in flower, soaring
yellow, overhung by smoke
from four white distant stacks – a gray
and violet stonelike swelling
in bright air.

3 Who lives
   in the house of gray splinters,
   with locust trees, with riven linen curtains
   stirred at a glassless window
   by air floating summer flax? A house
   beneath the scrapyard wall, the arm
   and great disc of the electromagnetic crane,
   the mounds of salvaged metal,
   orange and black: spiral shavings,
   crushed masses, pipes and cylinders,
   mazelike machine parts, stainless
   steel bored with long shining
   tubular hollows, and barbed
   tangles of wire. A house
   among flowering weeds, yellow
   gentian, the pink-white soapwort.
   A house near the eroded banks
   where thunderstorms or warm night rains
   lash or wash the rust
   down into the river.

4 People once of horses,
   of barges along rivers and canals
   grown over: now of rails
   rusting in fields, furnaces
   toppled on the stream bank.

   People of bitter, muscular sleep. Bound
   between cascading steel and blackened streams
   down from the coal mines over
   the rocks at Athens. Between
   wet clay, cheap pots, and a vast
   kiln's shell, falling,
   red ruin cut into the green
   steep banks of Ohio on the West
   Virginia side. By East
   Liverpool's empty frames. By apple-mounded
   Columbiana. In Newton Falls with cattle
   and slag mountains along the river.
   In Mesopotamia with the sound
   of a slow wind, ocean-wide,
   in stirring wheat, high up in oak and spruce.

   People who stopped a while to purge
   their acidic droppings
   in Mahoning. Pure restlessness, who shifted
   on pocked roads. Never enough,
   the loam's wealth, the oven's might. The streams
   always too narrow and too slow,
   streams of water in mosquito-burdened woods,
   of metal blazing up in black hangars.

   People dispersed by their own breath,
   blown beyond empire and beyond
   the quiet roof in waves of corn
   blazing with fireflies at dusk.

5 Once, late in a day, a gold came flooding down
from the end of a storm, but rose, too,
out of ditches, from among cattails and tiger lilies,
from shining leaves, wet asphalt
of the old highway
lost between farms, from roofs and crops.
And rose from the forgotten river glimpsed
beyond its screen of sycamore and willow.
That gold flickered up from the black
hidden water: a light,
but more a blood, as though pulsing
into fields, air, and sky
from Mahoning.

Then you drove on
to a red horizon, sunset
on steep ridges where once
the Bessemer converter's fire
outlasted day and night. And there
was Mahoning: the low sun
through weedy trees drew flame
from the black water in that valley
of hollow mills,
shells of furnaces, confusion
of rusted rails and scrap. With tackle and pole
along the tracks a man, old,
was coming back from the river:
stumbling on slag, he went, head bowed, attentive
to the struggle to place his feet
on the rotted ties.

ROAD INTO WARREN: SHIFT CHANGE

You came at night
with the road out of dew-rich fields,
out of mock clover, endless depths
of cricket song, to the glow
hovering in that hollow.

The air a rusted
fog, orange, lit from within:
it bathed with iodine,
burnt sulphur, floating acids
a city of black sheds,
black walls, doors that dwarfed
the men who went under
and within. 'We don't
live here. We come by turns
to keep it filled, that its work
be carried on. Some come – we come – at night
to vapour lamps and the blue-white flame, high up,
of vented gas burnt off. We pass
a chain-link gate, barbed at the top,
and its fringe of dusty blue
chicory, we walk under
long travelling cranes and ducts,
tank cars and the thousand blackened
windows, and go in.'

You drove on, and maples
came back to the roadside
and in the windshield stars
and the farmsteads'
distant lighted windows. Then
the road's long curve that descends
to Mahoning at a green bridge draped
in ailanthus and sycamore. The hidden
river sent up a deeper coolness
into the summer night, a sound
of smooth water-troubled rock,

and a white mist. The road turned then
to a long pitted street, you passed
broken sidewalks, dusty
lots and weeds, and three cars
at a stuccoed wall drawn up together
beneath a guttering buzz
of ancient neon: The Pink
Slipper, almost burnt out.

THE MEANDER

The leaden grains were already falling
then – but who
saw them? – from the great plumes,
burnished gray, deep violet, that bloomed
from stacks above the woods: bloomed softly
and rolled, spread, travelled in the sky,
torn and thinned on a spiralling
of slow air, in ancient summer.
Bright
smoke of the young mills
deepened in the Meander, clear
mirror, lithe stripling river,
and through their image
a boy – now
a long dead father – swam
naked. It is still possible to see him
there, by the stanchion of this concrete
bridge, under the sycamores.
He fishes with his hands,
his ankles divide the minnow school:
the air that floods,
cool, over the ridge,
brushes the heart-shaped scrotum,
the warm water shifts
the penis idly, when he lies back.

Dead one, bald forehead scarred,
infarcted heart, bold eye
that swam on graphitic liquid
while the lips told children
of long dead pleasure in the once
clear waters: will he
come back again, lie back
in the algae mass, the grove of cattail,
to watch the smoke: clouds of a sky
reshaped and coloured newly
for our evening?

MOSQUITO CREEK

To a stream
light flowing, liquid sound of night,
sparkling to relieve the
heavy, unmoving day, the cloak and kingship
and browning heat of August ...

to a dark stream your first
song attached its words. To a stream,
rapid, placid, clear,
a muscle of the earth, source
of pleasure. To a river
as eternal.

Now that song
knows
it shaped itself between stricken
breasts: festered creek, first
love, clogged vein,
thickening wound. There is a green
that veils the ancient threshold, the clear
surface. There is an old carp,
addled wanderer, gaping,
dazed, for breath on the broken
cement of a stair that sinks down
into the gray water.

Now that song is
remembering:
it proclaimed knowledge, once,
of unending freshness,
drawing from this stream its source.

Now it sings to itself:
you are not the one who began from fresh water.
You are not the one who can
declare again
as at first
the clean desire.

BONHAM WOODS, BANK OF THE MOSQUITO

Today was health
and empty sadness, empty
hands, under the bank,
hidden, in airy silences
veined with water sounds
and swallows. The sky
copied its colours, its calm
from the quiet of
the slashing wings. And far
within the moisture
of this borderland, the frogs: voices
as of water itself
belling to mate: unwavering song,
of comfort inconceivable in frigid
darkness, deepest content
in slime
under the pickerelweed.

Is there a way
through day, through evening?
The guide is wild. Just now
it pressed its furred head, small,
eager, against your palm,
you felt its breath.
Sleep-in-waking, it pants,
it butts your hand, runs off,
comes back to where you sit
unstirring, lies down by you.

And everything waits,
breathing slowly here. Night comes
along the silvered road of water
under oaks leaning
from the bank. Night,
motionless, the stars
repeating their steps again. This:
this is the way

to be going down the path.
The hour of bitterness, without air
or coolness, light or shade,
without warmth – don't let it be
the end of this day,
of my memory stretched now beneath
the tangled, untended
branches.

THAT YOU STILL LIVE

Scored, beaten, left
for dead here,
laid across these knolls
in the dust falling
from distant fires: leaf dust,
fine ash of sulphur, coal, burnt rubber,
plumes of smoke from the shredded
woods on the ridges.

Skin slobbered with the viscous,
rusty discharge of your wounds,
and the fall flies loud around
your drying blood,
and in it, caught, the burrs,
blown chaff and straw, carapaces
of the dead, all the refuse
of late fields, strips and chain-fenced lots
of weeds by the tar roads,
slag-beds of disused tracks.

You were still breathing
and though your wound obsessed the sight
of the one who found you, you were still pure
and rounded elsewhere, your body
preserved its long curving lines
that swept far away
to blue, to white. Unclothed
by the thieves who had fallen on you,
suffering, unconscious,
you were green openness asleep:
a breeze moving lightly along the streambed
parted the leaves, sun flashed
in secret water
purring below the fire-gold fields of stubble.

Still in love, had the murderers reeled away
from their half-finished task,
blessing their failure: that you
still live? And so
you are left here, racked
on the frame of the hills and gullies.

The witness, later,
came down by the same road.
Over the oak trees there were crows
harrying a hawk. He walked between
blackbirds watching on fenceposts,
finches on thistles. And saw you there.
And longed to step across,
to leave you and pass by
on the other side:
so terrified, so sickened he was
by your wounds – but you were still
more beautiful than broken, and your shuddering
breath still took in the wave, the endless
grid, of the fields and roads.

COUNTRY NEAR LAKE MILTON

Now the broken storm. All is
savagely tinted gold by a decaying
light – it seeps, liquid, from the curved gash
of clear sky above the corn horizon,
beneath the shattered clouds:
their hanging tatters, dragged
swiftly by the last of the wind,
sweep down along the roadside
trees and wires, the ditches
crowned with sweetpea.

Long road, empty and straight.
The setting sun, vast red,
and forays of crows, the bleak caws
falling in swollen silence
as separated droplets, the black beat
of their wings over the silver
silo, white gable, crumpled
roof of the unpainted barn – the far-off
fleeing wings another organ
of the dead calm.

Of all who have been unknown,
of all who were thrown out, poor,
into bypassed fields, or by
the roadside, was there ever
one who did not hate strengthlessly and call
down vengeance? Was there ever one who did not
die irrevocably
in dusk, alone, the moist hills
or glistening deserted streets,
light-swept after twilight storm,
his only, his muffling house?

The sun nests now and briefly stays
on the swell, on the feathered
tips, of the unripe hay
dust-green with water and new dark.
Over the surface of the grain a stirring
of air draws a white road.
Who comes? In the lone house
in the fields, who waits? Who sings,
O cool, sweet, empty, Ohio,
very faint, with leaves fluttering
in the moderate wind.

LOST CONTENT

You couples lying
where moon-scythes and day-scythes reaped you,
browning fruit falls and sleeps
in tangled nests, the wild grass,
falls from your apple tree that still grows here:
cry for your dead hero, his weak sword, his flight,
that you were slaughtered and your bed poured whiteness,
the issue of murdered marriage dawns.
The streets crack, a house falls open to the air,
sun and rain lie on the bed.
And the river still runs in a child's hands
under the factory's black hulk,
four stacks that used to bloom with smoke
over shining leaves, beneath thunderheads.
Then the storm
shatters and beats and after
in woods
a scented smoke of light,
a dripping quiet, and the small gold snake
sparkles at the pond's edge.
But who is he? What were
the goods he made, what became of his loved wife,
his children, and where
has he gone, fearsome, powerless? The silver
path of air from the river's bend to its rippling away
beneath the low concrete bridge
is still pure. No one comes, and the child
who watched by it has vanished.
Or sometimes he appears for a day, a night,
in the walls and windows reflected on the water,
in goldfinches' flight, cricket song, the heron's great
rise from the bank. Last a carp leaps,
voices and a lantern slide down the secret stream
in black and gold peace,
past the child's husk, the family never born.

NOTES AND ACKNOWLEDGEMENTS

Place names: the Mahoning River rises in northwestern Columbiana County, Ohio, flows northward through portions of Stark, Portage and Mahoning Counties, and into Trumbull County, where at Newton Falls it is joined by the West Branch, which rises to the west near Ravenna. The river then loops east and south, passing through the cities of Warren and Niles and – upon reentering Mahoning County – Youngstown. In Pennsylvania the Mahoning joins the Beaver River, which is a major tributary of the Allegheny.

The centre of Niles, my home town, is at the point where, nearly opposite each other, two creeks enter the Mahoning: the Meander from the south and the Mosquito from the north. My childhood home was near the Mosquito, which at that point is a river about fifty feet wide. Lake Milton, about twelve miles southwest of Niles, was produced by damming the Mahoning; Mosquito Lake and the Meander Reservoir are other nearby man-made lakes.

'The Faithful One': this poem is a monologue spoken by a painter who combines elements of many painters, such as Claude Lorrain, Goya and Rothko, and who also lives through – or comprises in himself – several historical eras. In each of the poem's 15 parts he describes and comments on paintings and drawings he has made, his artistic ideas and aims, and his experiences. The poem falls into three sections: parts I-V, childhood and adolescence; parts VI-X, maturity and professional achievement; parts XI-XV, old age and exile.

My thanks to those whose generous help with *Mahoning* led to many improvements: Theresa Moritz, Don McKay, Jan Zwicky, John Donlan and John Reibetanz.

Acknowledgements: 'Founders' was first published in *The Partisan Review*, 'City Plan' and 'East Wall' in *Pearl* (Copenhagen), and 'Given' in *Nimrod*. The writing of this book was made possible by fellowships and grants from the John Simon Guggenheim Memorial Foundation, the Ingram Merrill Foundation, the Canada Council, and the Ontario Arts Council. Special thanks to The Northrop Frye Centre of Victoria University in the University of Toronto: the

Centre's kind selection of me as 1993-94 Northrop Frye Visiting Lecturer was of great help in this project.

The cover photograph, by Theresa Moritz, shows the Fraternal Order of Eagles building on South Main Street, Niles, Ohio, near the south bank of the Mahoning River.

Interior photographs are from slides of Mahoning Valley steel mills taken about 1970 by Professor Albert F. Moritz, father of the author, to illustrate his lectures at Youngstown State University on pollution and ecology.

ABOUT THE AUTHOR

A native of Niles, Ohio, A.F. Moritz has lived in Toronto since graduating from Marquette University in 1974. He has been active as an essayist on poetry, as a reviewer, and as a translator, publishing six books from modern Spanish American and French poetry. He is the author, with his wife Theresa, of *Stephen Leacock: A Biography* (1985) and *The Oxford Literary Guide to Canada* (1987). His recent books of poetry include *Song of Fear* (1992), *The Ruined Cottage* (1993), and, with Ludwig Zeller, *Phantoms in the Ark* (1994). He has received the Award in Literature of the American Academy and Institute of Arts and Letters, and fellowships in poetry from the Canada Council, the Ingram Merrill Foundation, and the Guggenheim Foundation. Since 1986 he has taught literature and creative writing at the University of Toronto, where he is currently Northrop Frye Visiting Lecturer at Victoria College.